A Hilarious Moment!

Bringing sprinkles of laughter
to the heart and soul.

By Vera L. Smith

A wholly owned subsidiary of TBN

A Hilarious Moment!

Trilogy Christian Publishers A Wholly Owned Subsidiary of Trinity Broadcasting Network

2442 Michelle Drive Tustin, CA 92780

Rights Department, 2442 Michelle Drive, Tustin, CA 92780.

Trilogy Christian Publishing/TBN and colophon are trademarks of Trinity Broadcasting Network.

For information about special discounts for bulk purchases, please contact Trilogy Christian Publishing.

Trilogy Disclaimer: The views and content expressed in this book are those of the author and may not necessarily reflect the views and doctrine of Trilogy Christian Publishing or the Trinity Broadcasting Network.

Manufactured in the United States of America

10 9 8 7 6 5 4 3 2 1

Library of Congress Cataloging-in-Publication Data is available.

ISBN: 978-1-63769-582-1

E-ISBN: 978-1-63769-583-8

Dedicated to those who cherish
laughter and to those
who are learning.

Special Dedication to My Precious Grandson Victor

Many years ago, when I thought I had completed this book, my precious grandson Victor was still very young, and I had mentioned this book to him. But now, the years have passed while this book lay nestled warmly beneath my pile of written materials. Not too long ago, I added a few more hilarious moments that I felt were fitting to include in this book. It is Christmas time again (2017), and I have finally completed the writing of this book. For the second Christmas, Victor gave me another book to read (along with other gifts). While again leafing through the book he gave me last year *(Lillian's Right to Vote* by Jonah Winter & Shane W. Evans), I stopped again when I read the words he wrote inside the cover and thought to include his expressed words somewhere in this book. This is a good place. I was warmly reminded that I cherish the memories and laughter he gave me as a child. This is what Victor wrote to me:

12.24.16

"To my dearly beloved grandmother, you have been teaching me about our history since I was very young.

5

A Hilarious Moment!

Thank you for instilling your passion for education into me and for raising me with boundless love. You have inspired me to make a difference in the world for those society has failed. Thank you for teaching me to believe in myself. I love you with all my heart.

>*Merry Christmas!"*

— Grandson Victor

I thank you, Grandson Victor, for being a joy in my life and filling my heart with wonderful memories, precious moments, and laughter.

Dedicated to you too, Grandson.

With love,

Your Grandmother

6

Preface

As a youngster, I loved writing *and* drawing as my favorite pastimes, but I never knew such joyous things to do would bring me here to you. My life experiences have painted such vivid pictures in my heart and mind that the gift of writing and creative thought allows me to transfer these inspired skills to paper. This book is more than a book of hilarious real-life stories and stories about my own cherished memories, but it touches upon a few hilarious moments of others too, and this book even includes a little bit of history that can be awakening and refreshing to many readers. This book offers a family appeal. Not only can it bring families together to read and share funny stories that warm and refresh the heart, but this book will bring a period of reflective thought of the reader's own cherished memories that are sometimes lost to the busyness of life. My book, *A Hilarious Moment!* offers its own unique style of storytelling! The life stories will bring the reader on the road with me, the author. It is my hope that you, the reader, will bring to life my treasured and funny real-life stories to sprinkle the heart with laughter for such a time as this.

The Author

May 20, 2021

Acknowledgments

As with prior writings, this book has also been a solo project for me—one between God and me, so first of all, I acknowledge and thank God for the gift of writing and for taking the time to teach me along the way.

I thank those in my life whose memories were nestled deeply in my heart long ago to give me cherished and whimsical moments to now share with you, the reader.

I continue to acknowledge my sister-friend Neda, who told me years ago to "write a book, write a book, write a book." As you can see, my friend, I have not forgotten.

And I thank each reader for choosing my book to add to their own life story.

Finally, I believe we can all use slices of laughter as "good medicine for the soul," which words of wisdom have been inscribed in God's written word thousands of years ago.

Also by Vera L. Smith

Your Creation Declares Your Glory!

When God Spoke to Me, He Said...

Table of Contents

Foreword 15

Introduction 17

Chapter One—Laughter is Good Medicine! 19

The Funny Things We Do! 19

A Hilarious Moment! 22

Doggy Day! 25

Church Folk! 31

Chapter Two—Cherished Moments! 33

Strolling Down Memory Lane! 33

What We Did When We Were Kids! 38

Gone Are the Days When We Were Kids! 40

Chapter Three—Distant Memories! 45

Tribute to Al 45

Shark! 46

The Workplace Eavesdropper! 47

Mr. Motor Mouth! 48

Carl 50

Chapter Four—Slices of Laugher! **53**

Backward Flip! 53

Didn't See That Locked Door, Huh?! 55

Belly Laugh! 56

Through the Eyes of a Child 57

A Salute to Laughter! 59

Bibliography **61**

About the Author **62**

Foreword

" 'A Hilarious Moment' is a delightful and joyous read! It is well organized, scripturally saturated, well written, and an overall great read! The stories you share certainly bring a smile to readers as they get a glimpse into your world. You have a fabulous, uplifting spirit and perspective that shines through your writing."

—Ashley Welch, TBN

May 11, 2021

Introduction

The book, *A Hilarious Moment!* is riddled with humorous and cherished memories and amusing poetry written in a down-to-earth style that sizzle with laughter of sweet memories of times past that can rekindle cherished moments in the reader's own life while refreshing, hilarious moments enjoyed now.

Chapter One, titled "Laughter Is Good Medicine!" begins with a barrage of funny things we sometimes do in our own forgetfulness, like the time the author's friend absentmindedly put her shoe in an inconceivable place, which makes for a funny story! Chapter One also brings refreshment from quirky habits we sometimes hold on to that opens the door to whimsical moments worth sharing with others and to reflections of humorous moments when we don't see ourselves in action, but others around us do! This chapter is filled with moving poetry and humorous moments that are sure to warm and delight the heart!

Chapter Two, titled "Cherished Moments!" takes the reader on a stroll down memory lane, which is filled with showers of laughter that is good for the soul! With a small twist, this chapter applauds some of the old ways from the past that helped to shape young minds that need not be forgotten and discarded. Continuing its celebration of cherished and hardy moments of hilarity, Chapter Two brings to life heart-warming and cherished moments that are often long forgotten.

Chapter Three, "Remembering You!" combines hilarious life stories and comical tributes to others that tickle the eyes with laughter! The whimsical real-life stories in this chapter deliver humor to sometimes challenging moments by amusing characters such as Mr. Motor Mouth and The Workplace Eavesdropper! In this chapter, you will also find the story of Carl, whose amusing story inspired the book's cover.

Chapter Four, titled "Slices of Laughter!" brings this book to a heart-warming end! The real-life stories in this chapter continue their hardy applause to laughter, beginning with "Backward Flip!" where the author, following a veteran swimmer in four feet of water, experiences her own blunder that creates another hilarious moment! Chapter Four really does deliver slices of laughter with its comical life stories that tickle the heart! This chapter light-heartedly ends the book with the delightful story titled "Through the Eyes of a Child!" which brings the heart of the reader to a satisfying and calming end!

Chapter One: Laughter is Good Medicine!

The Funny Things We Do!

My friend Beverly said that I left her a message one morning about some forgetful things I had done in the past, and it made her chuckle. She said she thought about some of the same ole' silly things she'd done, like the time she couldn't find one of her shoes. She wanted to wear this particular pair of shoes to a job interview, but after looking all over her house for the one missing shoe, she gave up and reluctantly had to wear a different pair. It was later that afternoon when going to the refrigerator to grab something to eat, there laying as cold as a cucumber on one of the shelves in her refrigerator was her missing shoe! What funny things we sometimes do as we grow a bit older! Now another funny story.

The other day someone told me that their mother-in-law misplaced a set of keys, and after everyone looked all over the house for her keys, a curious thought led her son-in-law to look inside the microwave of all places, and you guessed it all right! Nestled as snug as a bug inside the microwave were his mother-in-law's keys! Now, what was this dear woman thinking—probably the same dreamy thoughts as my friend Beverly! Here's to my own absent-mindedness!

I had not too long ago moved into another house, so I was getting used to where things were. Take, for instance, the light switch in the garage and the garage door switch. I guess I must have been on automatic pilot when I flipped the garage door switch, thinking it was the light switch because my previous light switch was in the exact same spot on the wall where this current garage door opener is located. Although I caught myself this time, a few evenings ago, I didn't. One evening, I had gone inside the garage to look for something, and on the way out, I flipped a switch on the wall, thinking it was the light switch. Even after hearing the loud clanking sound the garage door makes when it is opened and closed, not paying attention, I walked right inside the house and closed the door behind me. You can imagine how shocked I was the next morning when I opened the door leading to the garage only to discover that my garage door was wide open, and the garage light was still on! With a huge slice of edginess, I quickly glanced around to see if anything was missing, and thank God; it wasn't! Not realizing what I'd done the night before, that following morning, I told my son that I had a faulty garage door opener that had somehow activated itself during the night and opened my garage door! My son Bryon tried to convince me that I must have left the garage door open, but

Chapter One: Laughter is Good Medicine

I swore up and down that I had closed it because I remembered I had flipped the switch on the wall before going inside the house. It wasn't until days later, when I reached for the light switch, that my hand landing on the garage door opener caused me to instantly realize that it was my own absent-mindedness that led to the garage door being left open that previous night. Before realizing what I'd done, for days, I would remove the battery from my garage door remote that hung on my sun visor, thinking it was faulty too. Totally embarrassed, I could never tell my son what I'd done, but now he'll know because he will read this book! You were right, Bryon! ☺

After moving into my new house, I had another funny thing happen. I just knew I had turned off the water faucet after washing my face one night, but when I got up the next morning, I noticed a small, steady stream flowing from the faucet. I thought to myself, *Now how did that happen?* I instantly had a disheartening thought about my next water bill. Sometime later, I was in the second bathroom and discovered the exact same thing—a steady flow of water, only this time the water hadn't run all night because I had gone back inside this second bathroom. Thinking again there was something wrong with the faucet handles, I thought to have them repaired. But after briefly pondering the design of the spigot handles that were totally different than the faucet handles in my old house, I knew the culprit was me! It's funny how we can get so used to things we've done in the past that we don't realize something similar can operate quite differently. I had to push the newer faucet handles rather than turning them like I used to do with my old faucet handles, which should have been a clear enough clue to me that something was off, but it slipped right on past me! Bon Voyage to our slippery absent-mindedness!

The Bible says that a happy heart is good medicine, and it is. Laughter promotes having a happy (joyous) heart, and one good thing about laughter is you can't be beset with woes and brimming with laughter at the same time. Someone told me the other day if you're feeling low, watch a very funny movie that makes you laugh! I think life is too short to feel melancholy more than you feel laughter. Now think of one of your fond memories that brings a smile to your face!

"A joyful heart is good medicine, but a broken spirit dries up the bones" (Proverbs 17:22, NASB).

The feeling of joy promotes laughter which vastly improves one's mood!

A Hilarious Moment!

You'll never believe what I just did,

while walking in my son Bobby's shoes that were *way* too big!

Around the corner and not looking as I went,

caught the toe of his big shoe on a board and down to the ground I was sent!

I couldn't help but yell out in agony,

as I quickly looked about for a neighbor, hoping they didn't see!

Nursing my scarred and bruised left knee,

I couldn't believe that ole ground had twisted me!

Upon my feet, I could barely stand.

I took off those ole' big shoes and threw them in the garbage can!

I learned my lesson, although I was somewhat shaken.

Nothing broken, but my poor body was aching!

While lying on the ground that summer day,

I couldn't help but remember what my youngest son did say!

"Mama, go ahead and throw these old shoes of mine away."

Now that would have saved me from this painful day!

A Hilarious Moment!

My son Bobby told me to throw away his old tennis shoes, but I didn't. I thought to myself, *these shoes will make good for working in the yard*! They were so big and comfy (size 13), I thought it was a good idea to keep these worn old shoes around. But, boy, was I ever wrong! My son's shoes were so big; I couldn't feel where my feet were landing or if I had cleared myself away from any pitfalls. Well, I learned one hot smoldering summer day, wearing shoes that are way too big is not such a good idea even if they are comfy!

The day I was wearing my son's shoes, it was a perfect day for working outside, and it was early enough, so I was ahead of the sweltering heat from a hot summer's day sun. I was carrying some tree trimmings to the garbage can on the side of the house, where there were several loose logs surrounding a small dirt area left there by the previous owners. Because the logs weren't mounted to anything, the logs would sometimes slip forward, and that's just what happened. One of the logs tumbled just far enough to catch the corner of Bobby's big ole' floppy right tennis shoe. With shoes that big, I never even felt that I had not cleared the log, so while trying to move forward, my foot got jammed against that small log, and down to the ground I went! It was like a comical explosion—me meeting the ground! I thought I was falling in slow motion, except, in reality, it was happening so fast that I couldn't even muster a single thought to cushion my fall, and just that quick, it was over!

Lying on the ground, a bit dazed, I immediately looked around to see if anyone was looking. Not spotting anyone, I fumbled to get up quickly before someone walked outside, except I couldn't move because my whole body was aching. I thought maybe something was out of whack, but a quick trip to the doctor's proved otherwise. Mostly, I suffered from a whole lot of embarrassment from a nasty ole' fall!

Yep, I learned something that day—don't walk so fast in shoes that are *way* too big because they have a mind of their own. As soon as I could stand up, the first thing I did was to kick off those ole' shoes and toss them in the garbage can, just like my son tried to tell me to do in the first place! I never looked back to the comfort of those ole' shoes. I'm okay now working around the yard in the comfort of my own worn-out tennis shoes! What a life-changing experience that was for me, and maybe it has been one for you too!

"He will fill your mouth with laughter, And your lips with joyful shouting" (Job 8:21a, NASB).

Doggy Day!

One hot, muggy summer day,

a neighbor of mine had a lot to say!

A Hilarious Moment!

Kneeling down working in his yard quite at peace and quite serene,

he suddenly felt hot breath on his neck—a Great Dane had arrived on the scene!

Ole' Mike was furious, as you might suspect!

He didn't like turning around and seeing a dog at his neck!

His body must have undergone quite a change,

because, after that day, things for Mike were never the same!

Has this sort of thing ever happened to you?

The unexpected arrival of a dog told you your yard work was through!

Well, Mike decided he'd better rig up a plan.

After that day, you'd see him working in his yard with his Rottweiler at hand!

Poor ole' Mike, I've experienced exactly what happened to you!

That Great Dane showed up when I was out working in

my yard too!

I just happened to be stooping down in my front yard one day,

when all of a sudden that dog was only ten feet away!

Such a huge dog, I instinctively got up and quickly ran!

I leaped over a three-foot-high retainer wall because I was much too afraid to stand!

"Oh, he won't bite; we're just out for a walk," my next-door neighbor said.

"How come you don't have him on a leash? His appearance fills us with such dread!"

Boy, was I shaken as I stood behind my front door screen!

"*You* know your dog, but to me, he looks awfully mean!"

I didn't know that I could move like that jumping over that retainer wall.

Though I stumbled and fumbled in my front yard, I did not dare fall!

A Hilarious Moment!

Whew! I thought whenever I worked out in my yard,

I think I'm gonna need a bodyguard!

Mike now has his big Rottweiler roaming over his land!

But God gave me quick feet and a front door close at hand!

I was walking down the sidewalk early one morning, and from round the bend, my eyes caught the partial figure of a person running. A bush was blocking my view, but I knew instinctively to look for a dog—*would it be on its leash?* I didn't know, so I starred quite intently because I wanted to be ready—me and my trusty ole' stick—just in case there was a dog without a leash! But when the man came in clear view, he not only had his dog on a leash, he even shortened the cord.

After this man and his dog passed by me, I thought of an incident I had with another dog that happened about ten years earlier which inspired my poem. Just the thought of this earlier incident makes me chuckle inside! Looking back, it is downright funny to me now.

I used to live next door to a very athletic young woman who owned a very large dog—a Great Dane. My neighbor down the street used to complain to me about this dog running loose while the owner jogged down the street. The first time I saw the dog, I was totally unprepared for what

Chapter One: Laughter is Good Medicine

I saw—his size was enormous! While working in my front yard, I was kneeling down picking up weeds and leaves out of a bed of white rock that lay at the base of a three-foot-high retainer wall when all of a sudden, out of the corner of my eye, I see this thing that looked like a pony except when I stood up and looked at it; it was a dog! He galloped his long muscly legs straight towards me as I headed straight for my front door! I jumped over that retainer wall and stumbled across the front lawn while I raced to my front door! I didn't take the time to look back because I figured a second might cost me a nip or two. From behind my screen door, I saw this humongous animal of a dog right there in my front yard. I couldn't believe what I had just narrowly escaped from! My neighbor called out, "Oh, he won't bite," as she called out to him while continuing her energetic jog down the street. One time I tried to explain to her that this was not a good idea, especially with the size of her Great Dane, so I was always peering around for her dog whenever I worked in my front yard because she continued to allow her dog to roam unleashed! I wasn't the only one who had a problem with this dog roaming around. My neighbor Mike who lived down the street had a problem with him too!

It was another hot summer day, and while out walking, I just so happened to head towards the other end of our court where Mike was outside working in his front yard. I remember seeing his Rottweiler lounging lazily on the front porch. As I got closer, Mike immediately started venting about feeling that Great Dane's hot breath on his neck while he was kneeling down to do some yard work. He said that he, too, was startled by the dog's size. Poor ole' Mike must have been so full of feelings behind what happened to him because he blurted out, "See my dog! That Great Dane came in my yard again yesterday, and my dog nipped at him and chased him away! That's what he'll get if it comes here from now on! I don't see why she walks him without a leash!" That's when I told him my story about jumping over my retainer wall when that dog galloped towards me. The day when Mike told me his story, he didn't laugh, and neither did I, but years later, I would laugh!

While walking home, I thought about Mike's story and had a sudden impulse to hurry home to write down the words of my poem while they were still fresh in my mind. I realize now that God had given me this special memory years earlier to record in a book that I would write many years later. Looking back, it was indeed a hilarious moment! This leaves me with only one other thing to say, "Hey, dog owners—put your dog on a leash, so you quit scaring folks like me!"

Just had a thought to add a P.S. Last Saturday, I went for a brisk walk in my neighborhood, and what did I happen to see a little ways down the sidewalk but a big dog trotting along with no leash, mouth open, tongue hanging out, but still looking like he could run a marathon! With no owner in sight, you know I turned around at lightning speed, so quick that I twisted my already sore right knee!

I tried to warn a bicyclist along my same path, but with earphones in his ears, I don't think he heard me because he headed straight for another doggy day!

Church Folk!

It's not their Sunday best

that tells you what's behind the scene.

It's when strife and stress come,

that you'll see what I mean!

Don't try to change their rules

they've followed for many years.

They'll challenge you to a showdown,

and you'll walk away in tears!

And when it's time for the Church to vote,

they go for the juggler, they go for the throat!

I had never seen such a wild display,

until I walked in church that day!

Surely I thought they'd have to apologize

before they continued their "call."

But when they walked in church again,

nothing was said—it was business as usual after all!

I looked up at the pastor,

thought surely he'd have them stand!

And let them know their ill conduct

was not fitting of a godly man!

Oh, pastor, man of God!

Take them by the hand!

When you see church folk acting up,

then you must take a stand!

Although this poem is included in my second published book, I think it adds a bit of humor now! Sometimes we can ponder our child-like behaviors and think, *was that really me*? Yep, that was you all right! That's what I say! We all have moments where we could have done things just a tad bit differently!

"…from the same mouth come both blessing and cursing. My brethren, these things ought not to be this way" (James 3:10, NASB).

Chapter Two: Cherished Moments!

Strolling Down Memory Lane!

Where I grew up at it was bitterly cold during the winter months. The ice that covered the sidewalks, front porches, and driveways made it pretty hard and sometimes downright comical to keep your feet on the ground *and* in the direction you're headed to. It was nothing to walk towards someone, only to slip and tumble right before you reached that person! Gazing out the back door window at folks walking by could bring some hilarious scenes to your eyes that would rip your insides apart with laughter! You'd watch someone raise a foot to step upon a porch, and then in a split second, you'd see them lying flat on the ground, looking around to see if anyone saw them fall. And someone always did! It was common for a neighbor to say to you, "I saw you when you fell down yesterday!" (Hee! Hee!)

One cold wintry day, I just so happened to go outside at the same time my dad was crossing the street. I knew as a kid we weren't supposed to laugh at the older folks, but that day I just couldn't help it. There was my dad wrapped from head to toe in his nicely lined trench coat, trying to keep warm while his feet were crisscrossing in fast motion and his legs flapping about in the icy air as he tried to keep from falling. Watching from the sidelines, I wanted to see who would win out—my dad's military agility or the icy breath of nature. While I watched him clutching his hat and trench coat, my dad hit the ground in style! And he did the same thing a few weeks later when he came out of a Kroger's grocery store. It was downright comical to watch his feet twist and turn on the icy surface as he fumbled to reach the doorknob of his parked car. Nature always seemed to win out because my dad went down in style again, meeting the icy and snow-covered ground with a thump!

Thinking of another memorable moment, one time my sister played a crafty trick on me in my growing up years. As a kid, you know how you looked up to your older siblings, and she knew this. We were in the living room when she told me to pretend to roller skate with her, so there we were, arms crisscrossed as we mimicked skating from side to side in our bare feet. I wondered why she insisted that I switch to the right side before we began to pretend roller skating, and I would soon find out why. It must have been one of the twins' cloth diapers that sprung a leak that landed baby poop on our linoleum floor, hidden from my view. Wouldn't you know that my sister made sure that my feet sloshed right through that poopy puddle as she glided me directly in its path! When I looked down and saw baby poop oozing between my toes, I cried out in disgust while my sister rolled with laughter as she looked down at my poopy-covered toes! She had completed her mission on her naive baby sister! I chuckle now, looking back at this moment, especially when I also remember one of my sister's own faux pas.

In our neighborhood, we had those old-fashion clotheslines in the backyard. They were made out of plastic rope that was tied between two poles. When it was dark outside, you really couldn't see the clotheslines, so you had to be extra careful to duck your head, or you'd run smack dab into one of them. One summery night this same sister who played that trick on me was playing outside with some of her friends, and wouldn't you know she ran smack dab into a clothesline that stopped her dead in her tracks! Seems I remember that she sort of hung there in midair for a few seconds before finally dropping to the ground. I saw her instantly grab for her throat. I didn't laugh then, but when she woke up the next morning with red circles all around the front of her neck, I did. But before you think poorly of me for laughing, my sister was more embarrassed than anything else! She never forgot about that old clothesline. What funny things we sometimes do when in our distractedness we forget something that was there all the time!

Then there is my brother Cooper. For a while, he lived with me and my boys when he moved out West. We used to go on walks together. My two young sons rode their bicycles, but sometimes my oldest son would ride his skateboard. Now, what did Cooper do one day but tell his nephew to let him try out his skateboard right while we were perched on top of a hilly road that spiraled downward? At first, Bryon said, "No, uncle Cooper, you might fall." But his uncle insisted to ride his skateboard when he said to my son, "Boy, give me that skateboard!" So my son gave his uncle his skateboard just like he said, and then we all silently watched as Cooper put one foot on the skateboard and instantly pummeled the ground (which saved him from a long downhill bumpy ride on his backside)! His unbalanced weight caused the skateboard to lunge forward, and we all burst out laughing, including my brother! He was an old dog trying to run with the little dogs but couldn't cut the mustard! ☺

Now my brother Skip loved to cook, and I believe his favorite dish was deep frying his homemade apple fritters. You'd see Skip in our kitchen jabbing at those apple fritters, trying to turn them as the hot oil had him jumping back and forth in true family style! But my brother hung in there and fought back by wrapping one hand in a kitchen cup towel while his other hand was drawn back as if in mortal combat. He never let go of his trusty spatula either in his wrapped hand as he flipped those fritters from one side to the other. Recently, when I asked him if he still knew how to make his apple fritters, I was surprised that he no longer remembered. The one thing he does remember, though, is to wrap his hand in a kitchen cup towel that he uses as weaponry against hot popping oil! Not too long ago, his wife Ruby laughingly told me, "Yep, he still wraps his hand in the old-fashioned style!" Now on to another hilarious moment!

Years ago, my sister Dee bought a sharp-looking two-seater sports car from a used car lot. You'd see her flitting around town with the convertible top down. It must have been past the thirty-day grace period when she started having trouble with her little sports car. One day when it stopped on her, she got out to raise the hood to see what the problem was. To our horror and surprise, there written in bold lettering on the greasy underside of the hood was the word, "Lemon." What some folks won't do for a dollar!

On another hot summer day, one of my younger sisters and I were on our way home. We were both fearful of stray dogs, so when we heard the sound of a dog's clawed paws hitting the hot pavement, we quickly looked back, saw that a dog was running full speed in our direction, thinking it was surely coming to get us, we grabbed each other's arm and instinctively took off running. We both eyed the hood of somebody's parked truck, and you should have seen us scrambling to get on top of the hood! But the dog ran right on past us as though he didn't see us. And there we stood like kings on the hood of someone's truck with our adrenaline pumping, just waiting to fend off a dog that never even looked our way. What a treasured and relieved summer's day!

"The memory of the [uncompromisingly] righteous is a blessing…" (Proverbs 10:7a, AMPC).

What We Did When We Were Kids!

Hopscotch, jump rope, and double dutch!
These were the games we loved so much!
Making green salad from the grass!
And the mud pies—we ate them last!

Pretend to be grown-ups so we can play
mom and dad with kids for a day!
Clear out a flat space in some dirt,
you lost your best marble—oww, that hurt!

Going to the playground so we can swing!
See who can go the highest—now that was the thing!
Run home fast before the day was done—
this is what we did when we had fun!

Our growing-up days were filled with fun and laughter.
We played marbles, double-dutch, two square, four square,
red light, green light, and play house. And let me not forget
playing jacks. So many wonderful things we did to have
fun!

Chapter Two: Cherished Moments!

My granddaughter Jade told me the other day that now-adays, kids like to stay indoors and play games on their tablets. She said she's never played marbles before and certainly no pretend eating green salad made from grass and mud pies made from water and dirt! With no playing the game of marbles, kids don't know the art of winning and losing prized possessions all in good ole' fashion competition.

I think today, most kids are missing out on much of what the outdoors has to offer. They are missing out on using their imaginations to come up with creative things to do while having fun outdoors. The good ole' days may seem antiquated, but they worked. Kids learned community behaviors that are not seen much today. They learned sportsmanship and what it means to share with one another good-naturedly, although sometimes we had small skirmishes where the most thing that was hurt was our feelings. I watch sometimes how my grandkids fuss over things, and you probably see this too. But if we were caught arguing, we were told to work it out. Today I see parents investing in things for kids to play with instead of investing in kids to use their God-given imaginations.

My cultural history is filled with the richness of creative ideas that were embedded in young minds that made this country great. From Morgan Garrett as a young boy building stick playthings and later inventing the traffic light to George W. Carver creating lotions and soaps and peanut butter, kids back then were thrust into a learning environment that led to something greater for the world we live in today. We should not forget this, and we should work to awaken greatness in this generation of youngsters to accomplish things that matter most.

One thing I do see is kids still having fun on the playgrounds. The swings, the monkey bars, and the sandbox were favorites when we were kids! We had neighborhood centers where we could check out play equipment too. Admittedly, the neighborhoods back then were a lot safer, so a bunch of us kids would hang out at the playground practically the whole day, or we would gather together to play in someone's front yard. I shared with my granddaughter how we used to get an old blanket and have one of our playmates lay in the middle while two of us grabbed opposite ends of the blanket, and then we would swing our playmate back and forth from side to side, sometimes thumping their bottom on the ground because of us laughing so hard we'd lose our grip! Gone are the days of seeing the fun things we did when we were kids!

Gone Are the Days When We Were Kids!

When we were kids, we did simple things for fun.

Like catching tiny drops of rain on our tongues!

Chapter Two: Cherished Moments!

Run bare feet on the paved streets!
On to the corner store to buy some sweets!

Those were the days when neighbors cared—
from their cupboards, they would share.
Go to "Miss Lady" to borrow an egg.
If hungry, a kid would not have to beg.

Everyone knew who was your kin.
Lose your child, they'd bring him home again!
And if they saw you doing something wrong,
they'd yell for your father when he got home!

Gone are those days when we were kids.
Gone are the days of the simple things we did!
Now only living in our hearts—
those cherished memories will never depart!

At the time I wrote this poem, I must have really been
reminiscing my childhood years because this is the second
poem written about those treasured moments. It was a lot
of fun we had back then, and those cherished memories still
live on.

A Hilarious Moment!

I believe the simple things in life are the best things to enjoy. As a youngster, we used to catch tiny drops of rain on our tongue for fun, and we played Rise Sally Rise. We had a rhythmic way of clapping our hands in tempo to our childhood song, "Take me Back to the Ballgame"! In our neighborhood, we had a small corner store called Mr. Otis. "Let's go to Mr. Otis," we'd say, "to buy some candy or a bottle of pop" (okay, soda pop or just plain soda!). I remember my dad saying, "Go borrow an egg from Miss Lady" (across the street). Back then, neighbors would borrow small things like an egg or a cup of sugar from each other, and we never actually paid it back because sharing with each other was understood. Things like that kept us close as a community. And don't do something wrong because as soon as your father got home, a neighbor would meet him out in the front yard and tell on you! Grown-ups respected each other, and we respected them too. The first time I heard a cousin of mine's kids address him and his wife by their first name, I thought, *Wow, how strange*! I tried to wrap my head around that because we never would dream of addressing our parents on a first-name basis. The world has changed so much from when we were kids, and not all of the changes are for the better. I believe some of the old ways need to remain untouched because they work. The beauty of it all back then is people in communities really looked out for each other. And true to what I wrote, if a child was lost, a neighbor would drive you home to your parents. Gone are those days when we were kids, like

Chapter Two: Cherished Moments!

catching tiny raindrops on our tongue! ☺ Long gone are the days of the simple things we did. Now only living in our hearts, those cherished memories will never depart.

Chapter Three: Distant Memories!

Tribute to Al

To my friendly coworker Al, whose love for the water—even shark-infested waters made me afraid for him. One day while at work, I listened to one of Al's shark stories, and it was all that I could take! I went back to my desk, and moments later, I had pecked out a poem and handed it to him. I didn't think much of it and even signed it "Author Unknown" because I didn't realize then he would think much of my poem. Boy, was I wrong! Al was so elated over my poem that he called his girlfriend and read it to her over the phone. I laughed because I only gave him this poem as a funny gesture, but in a sincere way, I was telling him to be more mindful of who has the most authority in the water—the shark does! As I turned to leave his cubicle, I saw him pin my funny little poem on the wall of his office cubicle. He said he was going to keep it so when I become an author, in public, he would say, "Hey, I know that woman! She wrote me a poem!" My poem to Al:

Shark!

Sharks are very beautiful,

but also deadly too!

Stay out of their water, Al

or they'll come after you!

Be wise—beware of where you are!

If not, Al, you won't get very far!

Appreciating something is hardly the same

as putting yourself in danger—

now that's a crying shame!

I almost forgot! The same day I gave this poem to Al, he asked me if I could write another poem, a poem that he wanted to give to his supervisor. He then explained to me that his supervisor was bugging him, and he wanted a poem to address the issues he had with him. To Al's request, I replied, "Yes, I could do that, but *no* way!" I had done something similar with a very disruptive coworker from my past, and I remember sweating it out for days, hoping no one would discover it was me who wrote that poem and placed it in her mailbox. No thanks, Al!

Added Note. Many years later, after writing this poem

to Al, I tried to think back to the job where we met, but I could only remember writing this poem to him. Musing over Al's personal comment to me, I sorely wish I knew where it was that we had worked together. He's probably out there somewhere, but where, I don't know—a tribute to you, my past coworker Al wherever you are.

"For wisdom will enter your heart, And knowledge will be pleasant to your soul" (Proverbs 2:10, NASB).

The Workplace Eavesdropper!

The workplace eavesdropper—what a pesky little creature! He knows the latest news and all the details before you do! If he just happens to be sitting on the other side of your cubicle wall while you're talking on the phone, don't be surprised if he butts right in to give you his opinion or maybe to answer a question or two about the personal conversation you're having with someone else! Tis true, tis true, I tell you! And if you try to speak in a softer voice to keep him from listening in, it's not beneath his dignity to walk right in on you. He "accidentally" drops a piece of paper in front of your cubicle so as not to miss any important details. Now just how long does it take to pick up one sheet of paper?! It gets even better when after you've ended a phone call, he comes right over to continue that phone conversation with you!

And don't stand near the water cooler to have a private

dialog—the eavesdropper is always quite thirsty right about this time! And don't be shocked if you haven't finished your conversation with a friend to his satisfaction because he just might approach you while you're sitting quietly at your desk to say, "Do you still have that problem with your neighbor?" Or, "Did your husband ever get around to confronting his boss?" You feel like asking the eavesdropper, "How do you know about all of this?" But you don't because you know his line of work—eavesdropping! Women, the next time you decide to retreat to the ladies' room to have a private conversation, be sure to take a quick peek under each stall. You might just want to take a quick peek over the top too because there hunched over the commode with high-heels on and all you, just might find a "good" eavesdropper!

Laughingly recorded from true workplace incidents, except for the potty one! ☺

Mr. Motor Mouth!

If you can keep him quiet just long enough to tell him it's time to say good night, you've done well. Mr. Motor Mouth—you can hardly get him to quit talking or to slow down on what he's saying! At first, his conversation starts off interestingly enough, but then it drags on and on and on while you sit there watching the clock, just waiting for this unexpected visitor to go home.

It never fails; you're in a hurry and look who's coming your way—Mr. Motor Mouth! You try to quickly dart around the corner without being seen, but too late, he saw you! Your feeble attempts to quickly end the conversation fail. He is not listening, only talking. Good, here comes a neighbor. You fake a conversation just long enough to get away from Mr. Motor Mouth!

Home from work, at last, you know, every Friday evening, Mr. Motor Mouth just "happens" to be in the neighborhood. Pull the shades down quickly before you're seen! Your sister calls and says she's bringing over a dish she borrowed from you. You hesitate but decide you need it to bake a casserole tonight. The doorbell rings, and when you open the door, in walks your sister with Mr. Motor Mouth trailing behind! What bad timing! After your sister leaves, you find yourself stuck another Friday night with Mr. Motor Mouth. You sit quietly, offering a word or two every half hour or so, and this doesn't seem to bother him at all. You cook, you clean; he continues to talk to you from the other room. You finally sit down and lean sleepily against the sofa. Maybe he'll get the hint and leave. Nope, didn't work! You lay your head on the arm of the sofa. Still, this doesn't work either. You glance at the clock. It's been three hours. You mention that you have to get an early start tomorrow. By now, your eyelids are getting heavier and heavier. Finally, you doze off for a few seconds, then suddenly you awaken with eyes wide open, startled that you've actually fallen asleep! You sit up rather quickly. He didn't even notice because he never stopped talking. At last, he yawns and decides it is getting pretty late; maybe he should be going on his way, he says. The door closes behind him, and you wonder, *what will I do next Friday evening*? You decide, sister or no sister, I'm not opening my door! Tis a true story!

Carl

What is it about our work Carl, that makes you dash away?

When it seems so clear to me, you have such wonderful ability—that's what I'd always say.

I'll hold your hand while gently nudging you to understand Carl,

all the work you see is really something you can do!

You've mastered a rigorous school program, so I know laying deep inside

is the key to releasing your ambition that need not be justified.

You surely have been a nice person to work with, Carl

although I finally had to see,

when it comes to our teamwork assigned—

"*I* got this! For God has given me a wonderfully capable mind!" ☺

50

Chapter Three: Distant Memories!

Years ago, I really did work with a very nice gentleman. Comically illustrated on the cover of this book, he would all but pass out at the sight of work assigned to our two-person team. I don't know what it was about our project that made him feel queasy, but boy, can we sometimes allow our thoughts to get the best of us! Hopefully, whenever my former coworker recalls us working together, he will remember his valor and wit to have earned a Master's Degree, and he will ponder our time together with fond memories. Smart cookie you are, Carl! That's what I would say! (Real name not used.)

"I will give thanks to Thee, for I am fearfully and wonderfully made" (Psalm 139:14, NASB).

Chapter Four-Slices of Laugher!

Backward Flip!

I thought my little book was finished, but there are just a tad more hilarious moments that we can enjoy!

Not too long ago, at a water aerobics class one Saturday morning, we had a new instructor filling in for our regular instructor, and boy did she have us twisting and turning in the water to her oldies but goodies music! Loved it! But then she told us to take our noodle, submerge it under the water, and paddle backward. Now I was doing just what she said when along came this veteran swimmer who floated on her back using her noodle while she kicked her feet as she moved effortlessly to the other side of the pool. Being a mediocre swimmer, it still looked easy enough for me to do, so I thought I'd give it a try. Well, you can probably guess what happened. Almost instantly, I flipped over! Something went sideways with my noodle, and the next thing I knew, I was on my face going down in the water, struggling to keep my head afloat. I think I must have flipped over at least three times as I fought to get my feet

on the bottom of the pool! When I finally got myself up-
right, the first thing I did was to feel on the top of my head
to make sure my fake ponytail was still attached and wasn't
hanging off the side of my face. My glasses had flown off
somehow, and I didn't even know they were missing until
the veteran swimmer told me that she was going to dive
down to get my glasses. That's when I felt my face, and
yep, they were missing all right! I was so stunned, embarrassed, and pretty much befuddled because I just couldn't
believe what had just happened to me! By this time, the
instructor had rushed over to my side, bent down, and
asked me if I were okay. The only thing I could do was
nod my head because I couldn't talk—too stunned. And
then I looked around the pool and saw that everybody had
stopped what they were doing and was just staring at me,
probably in disbelief! Moments later, I laughed at my own
absurdity! ☺

Guess what my first thought was after it was all over?
Well, I'll tell you. After composing myself, the first thought
I had was, *I wish someone would have caught this on video.
I think it would have gone viral!*

P.S. Just so you know, I got a thing about falling backward in water even if it is only four feet deep. You too?! ☺

Didn't See That Locked Door, Huh?!

I was at work one morning watching for folks entering our center when all of a sudden, this man, with quite a deliberate stride, walked inside the front door and headed straight towards a very obviously key padded locked door that knocked him instantly backward! I had to laugh as he "rubbed a dubbed" his forehead with a bewildered look pasted across his face! In total amazement of his faux pas, I said, "You just walked into that door!" Boy, was I glad that he just smiled back and replied, "I know!"

And just in case you're wondering why I didn't stop him before his blooper, his deliberate gait told me that he knew exactly where he was going, so I watched as he smacked into that locked door *and* on the side where the hinges are, and not on the doorknob side. Later that afternoon, he came back into our center, and I said to him, "Aren't you the one?" while pointing at the key padded locked door. He mumbled, "Uh-huh," as then gave a small chuckle! What silly things we sometimes do even as grown-ups!

A Hilarious Moment!

Belly Laugh!

One morning, while sitting in a chair in my coworker Joe's office, I was half-listening while another co-worker told him about her honey qualifying for a senior rental with a very low monthly cost. I thought I heard her say something about income, but by that time, I was already dialing the number to the apartment complex. When the woman on the other end of the line told me the income limit was 3500, I said, "$3500 a month!?" (I knew I was in!) But then she said, "No, $35,000 a year." (*Hmmmm, don't recall hearing her say anything about thousands.*) Sitting in his office chair, my co-worker Joe must have heard me say to the woman on the other end of phone with a measure of alarm in my voice after I repeated the word $35,000, "Well, I'll starve and be on the street!" because that's when I heard a muffled sound coming from his direction. When I turned my head to find out what that sound was, the only thing I saw was the left side of Joe's face, his left arm, and the left side of his belly shaking hysterically with laughter while he tried to restrain himself. He was cracking up because of what I had just to the woman on the phone. Guess this is why folks tell me that I have a funny way of saying things that makes people laugh. I naturally tell it like tis, and most times, it comes out with a hint of whimsical humor!

Through the Eyes of a Child

Kids are funny little creatures, and they say and do some of the darnedest things! Like this bright-eyed and witty-looking little person who waltzed right inside our agency with her mother. Immediately she took to me, so I fetched a coloring book and some crayons to keep her busy while her mother pecked away on a computer. Sitting down at a computer myself, this little one slides in close to me, so I asked her what her name was. With a slight thickness of tongue, I heard "Thia" (but later, her mother told me her name is Dia). I asked if she could write her name, and without so much as a hesitation, she said, "Uh-Huh," as she nodded her head. Now, this is the funny part—she instantly sought for a piece of paper and a pencil on the desk in front of us, and when she spotted a small stapled pad of paper as if she knew what she was doing, she casually flipped through the first blank sheets and then stopped when she saw some preformatted images and text on one of the sheets of paper. In an adult-like fashion, she tightly folded back the blank pages and became busily absorbed with writing her name. So impressed by her impetuous response to my request, I just knew I would see her name sprawled in child-like letters across a blank space on that small sheet of paper. Well, I saw it all right, but it was written through the eyes of a child. Her name was written through the eyes of a confident and dainty three-year-old, which I later discovered to my surprise! What stared back at me from that pad of paper was perfect child-like scribble–

Astonished, the only thing I could think to say was, "Is this your name?" With a smirk painted across her small, laughingly clinched lips and a twinkle in her eyes, she announced to the world, "ooh-wee! I just done something nice!" I had been fooled by a 3-year-old's impeccable behavior!

P.S. When talking with a little person, we must become a little person too!

We just might stand a chance then at not being outwitted!

"You have put more joy in my heart than they have when their grain and wine abound" (Psalm 4:7, HCSB).

A Salute to Laughter!

There are many benefits to laughter—a countenance of merriment, a rekindling of brighter moments, a refocusing of thoughts, a tension reliever, and the drawing together of family and friends, which are among the numerous benefits of laughter. Laughter can erupt from storytelling, the sharing of special moments, and cherished memories of long ago. When it comes to hilarity that tickles the eye of the heart, pause and consider—laughter is universal, the cost is free, and it brings a smile on the faces of those we know and those we've never met. Here's to your joy in reading *A Hilarious Moment!*

Bibliography

1. Winer, J. & Evans, S.W. *Lillian's Right to Vote.* Schwartz & Wade, 2015.

2. Ryrie, C. C. *The Ryrie Study Bible: New American Standard Bible.* Chicago: The Moody Bible Institute, 1976.

3. Amplified Bible, Classic Edition. (AMPC) (1987 ed.).

4. Holman Christian Standard Bible (HCSM). Copyright 1999, 2000, 2002, 2003, 2009.

5. Neighbor Mike, quote.

6. Son Bryon, quote.

7. Grandson Victor, quote.

8. Brother Cooper, quote.

9. Sister-in-law Ruby, quote.

10. Neighbor Darleen, quote.

11. Little girl Dia, quote.

12. Co-worker Al, quote.

13. Friend Beverly, mentioned.

14. Co-worker Joe, mentioned

About the Author

Vera L. Smith began writing as a youngster. Initially writing from experiences that beset her life or the life of someone close to her, Vera would capture a penetrating life message between the lines of witty poetry. Today, she continues to captivate her readers with personal real-life stories woven between the lines of invigorating poetry and biblical scripture. Vera has a great admiration for writing that provides medicine for the soul that emboldens spiritual, mental, and emotional well-being and moral thinking. Her writing captured in the book, *A Hilarious Moment!* leaves the reader with the rekindling of cherished memories long to be remembered. Vera graduated *summa cum laude* ("with highest honors") in a Bachelor of Science degree program where she majored in Psychology. Her poem, "The Mighty Waves of the Ocean," published in her first book, won the International Library of Poetry's Distinguished Honor Award. Vera has also earned a substitute teaching credential along with two other credentials. Earlier in her career, her passionate delivery in public speaking opened the door to recite the late Dr. Martin Luther King Jr.'s "I Have a Dream" speech for Black History Month at Travis AFB. As an African American, in her youth, Vera also competed and won the role of Snow White in a sixth-grade play. Vera's life journey reminds us that dreams can be born at any season of life. "So, keep moving forward," comments the author.